Superhero Superstars
Chadwick Boseman

by Emma Huddleston

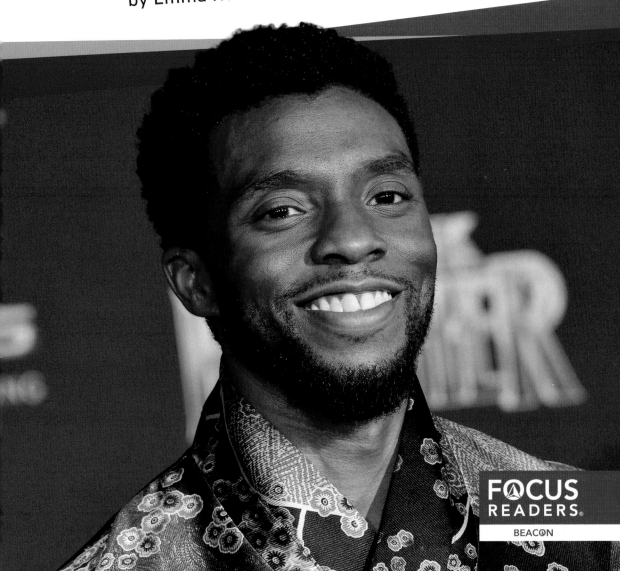

FOCUS READERS.

BEACON

www.focusreaders.com

Focus Readers is distributed by North Star Editions:
sales@northstareditions.com | 888-417-0195

Produced for Focus Readers by Red Line Editorial.

Photographs ©: Sthanlee B. Mirador/Sipa USA/AP Images, cover, 1; Shutterstock Images, 4, 8, 11, 19, 25, 27, 29; Marvel/Splash News/SplashNews.com/Newscom, 6; Cheriss May/Sipa USA/AP Images, 12; Rogelio V. Solis/AP Images, 14; Bernard Troncale/The Birmingham News/AP Images, 17; AF Archive/Marvel Studios/Disney/Alamy, 20–21; Matt Sayles/Invision/AP Images, 22

Library of Congress Cataloging-in-Publication Data

Library of Congress Cataloging-in-Publication Data is available on the Library of Congress website.

ISBN

978-1-64493-366-4 (hardcover)
978-1-64493-442-5 (paperback)
978-1-64493-594-1 (ebook pdf)
978-1-64493-518-7 (hosted ebook)

Printed in the United States of America
Mankato, MN
082020

About the Author

Emma Huddleston lives in the Twin Cities with her husband. She enjoys writing children's books and reading mystery novels. If she could choose a superpower, it would be to read other people's minds.

Table of Contents

CHAPTER 1

Black Panther 5

CHAPTER 2

From Writing to Acting 9

CHAPTER 3

Telling Stories That Matter 15

 **INSIDE HOLLYWOOD**

Black Panther Costumes 20

CHAPTER 4

The World of Wakanda 23

Focus on Chadwick Boseman • 28
Glossary • 30
To Learn More • 31
Index • 32

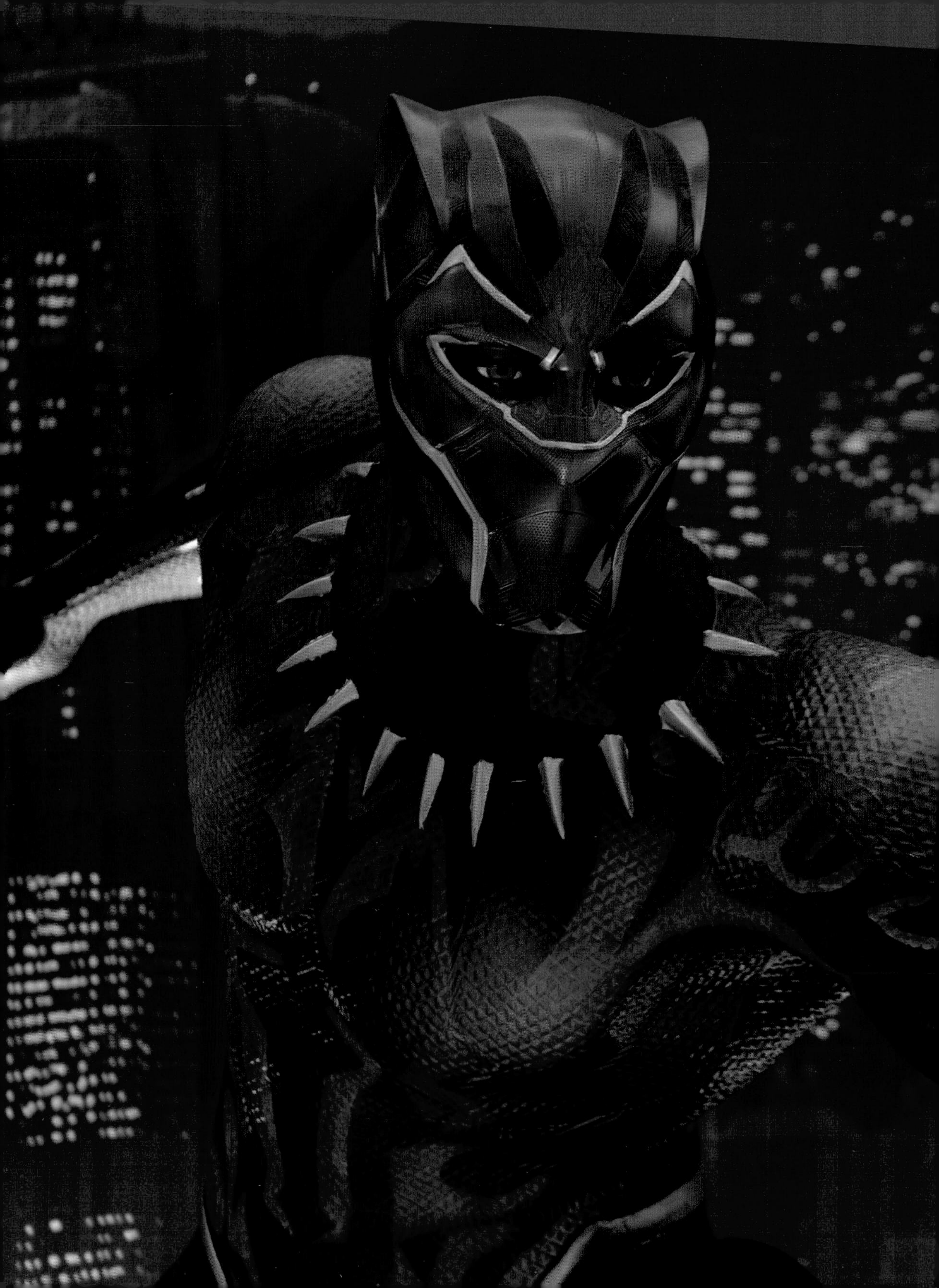

Chapter 1

Black Panther

Black Panther crouches on top of a car. His fingers grip the roof. His sister Shuri is driving the car. Black Panther and Shuri are chasing a **villain**.

 Black Panther's suit is bulletproof and has claws made out of vibranium.

 In 2018, Black Panther's sister Shuri got her own comic book series.

Shuri drives fast and steers carefully. The street is crowded. Shops line each side. People walk on the sidewalks.

Black Panther holds on tight. He watches the car ahead. He waits for the right moment to pounce. Then he jumps. He reaches his arms out to the villain's car.

Suddenly, Chadwick Boseman lands on soft padding. The actor plays superhero Black Panther in a movie. He was filming a car chase. The scene is one of the movie's many **stunts**.

Fun Fact

Boseman earned $2 million for his acting in *Black Panther.*

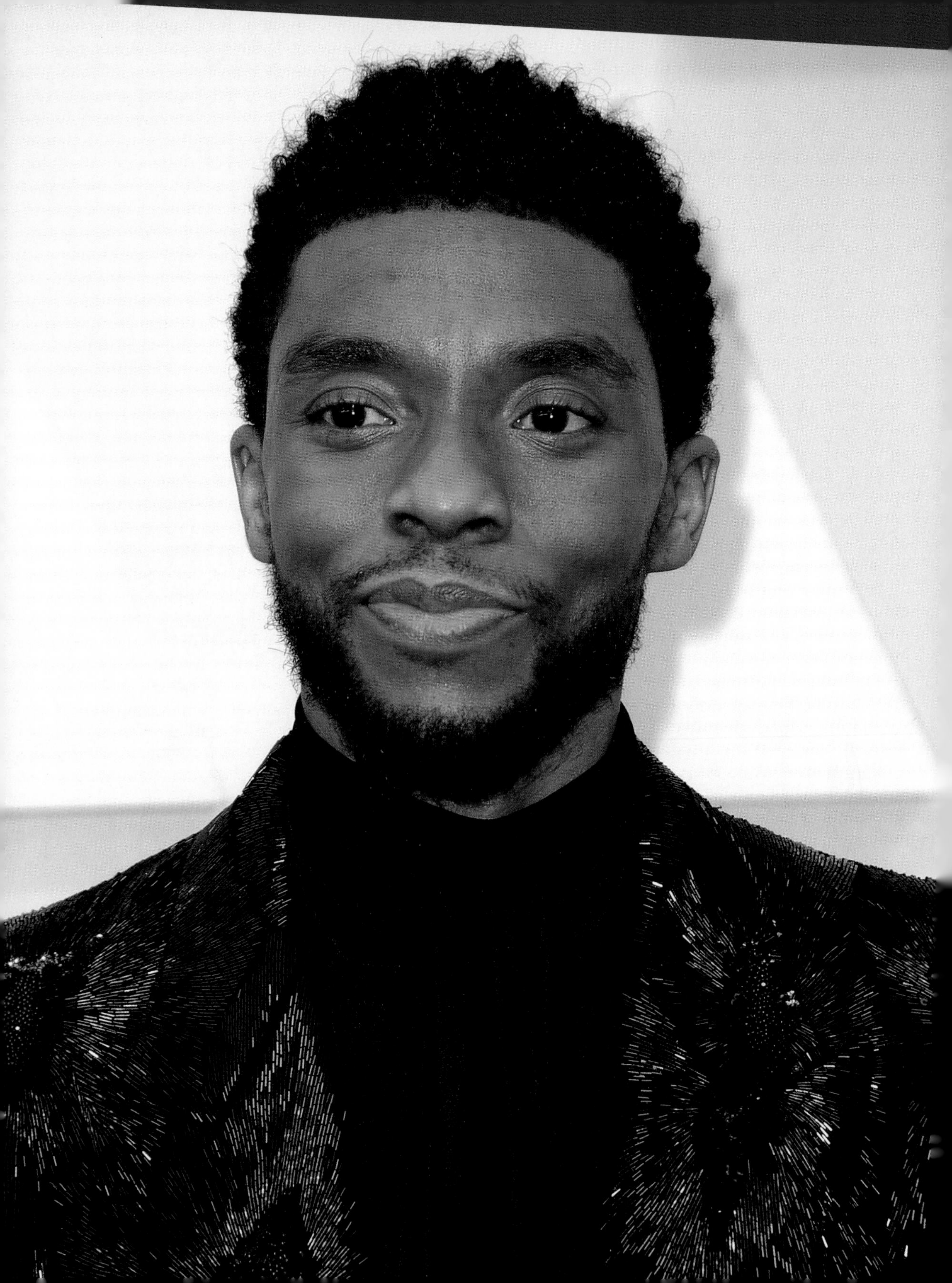

Chapter 2

From Writing to Acting

Chadwick Boseman was born on November 29, 1977. He grew up in Anderson, South Carolina. His father worked at a clothing factory. His mother was a nurse. He has two older brothers.

 Boseman was a writer and director before he began acting.

Chadwick enjoyed playing basketball. But he realized he liked telling stories more. In high school, he wrote his first play. It was called *Crossroads*. He **staged** it at his school.

In college, Boseman studied to be a **director**. He graduated from Howard University in Washington,

Fun Fact

Boseman still plays basketball for fun. He also enjoys boxing.

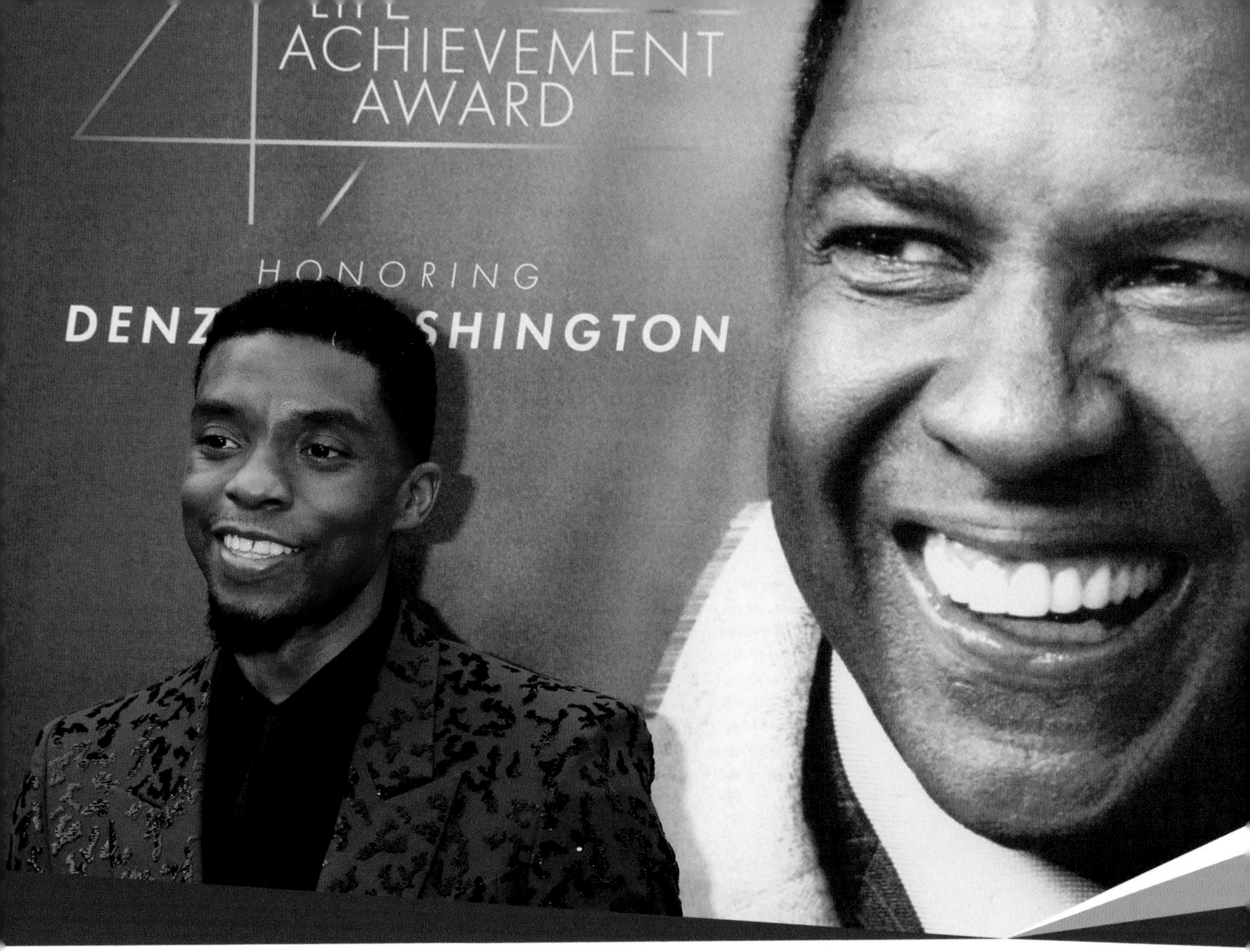
ACHIEVEMENT
AWARD
HONORING

Boseman honored Denzel Washington when Washington received a major award in 2019.

DC. After that, he took part in a theater program in England. Actor Denzel Washington paid for Boseman to go.

 Boseman returned to Howard University to speak at the 2018 graduation ceremony.

Boseman moved to New York City in his early 20s. He wrote and directed plays. He taught acting lessons for kids. Boseman also started acting himself. He wanted to know what acting was like. He thought it would make him a better director.

Boseman acted in many plays. He won a theater award in 2002. In the mid-2000s, he was in several television shows. Boseman's acting skills grew. He received bigger roles. Before long, he appeared on the big screen. He acted in a movie for the first time in 2008.

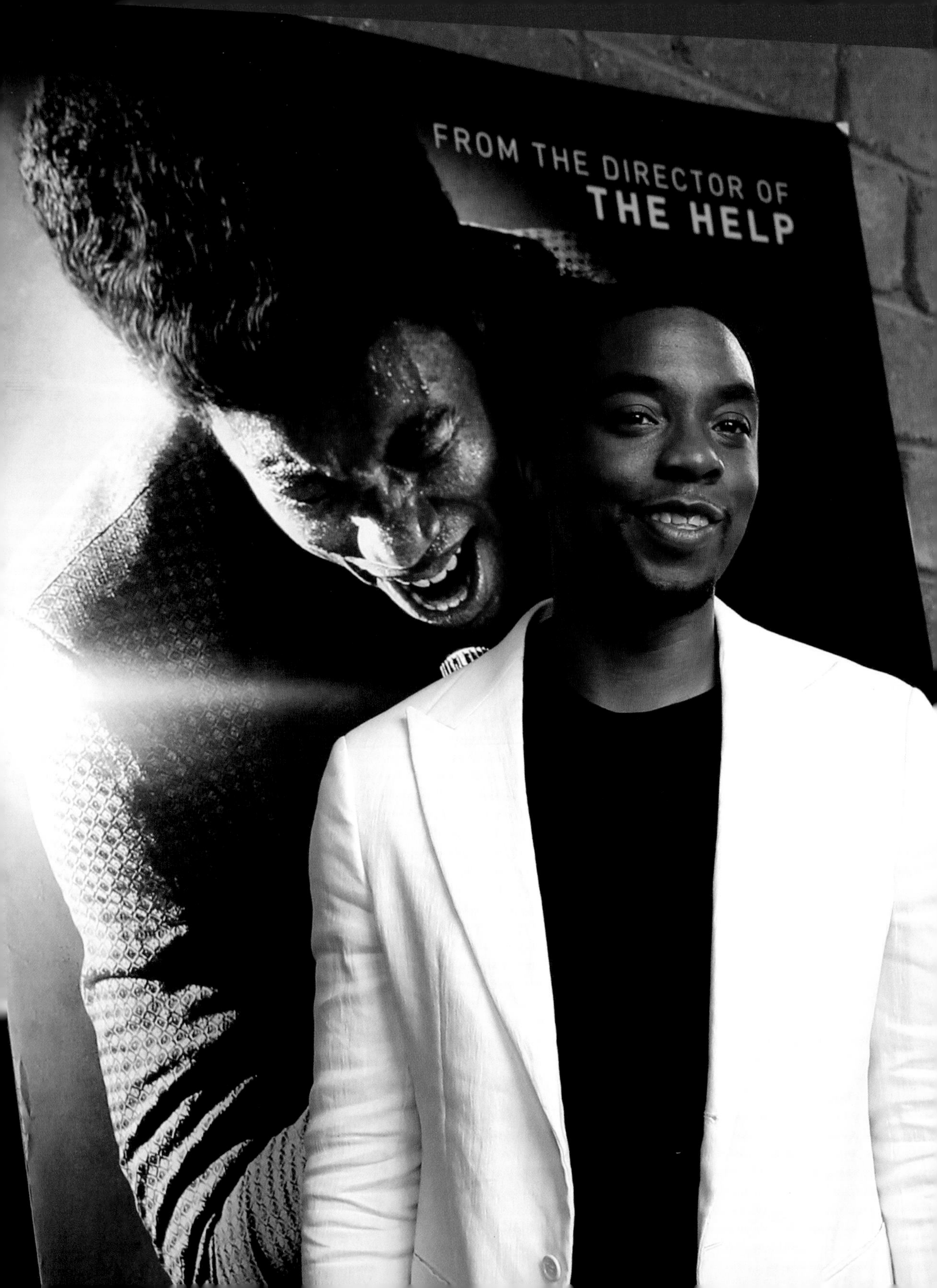
FROM THE DIRECTOR OF
THE HELP

Chapter 3

Telling Stories That Matter

Boseman's first movie was *The Express* in 2008. His character was football player Floyd Little. Little was a teammate of Ernie Davis. Davis was the first black player to win the **Heisman Trophy**.

Boseman played the singer James Brown in a 2014 film.

Boseman is known for playing characters based on real people. He often plays people who made a mark in black history. For example, he played Jackie Robinson in a 2013 movie. Robinson was the first black player in modern Major League Baseball.

Fun Fact

Boseman played Thurgood Marshall in 2017. Marshall was the first black justice on the US Supreme Court.

 Boseman played Jackie Robinson in a movie. Robinson joined the Brooklyn Dodgers in 1947.

In addition to acting, Boseman still writes. He continues to tell stories. He focuses on black history. He says many stories of black Americans have not been told yet.

He knows he has the chance to tell some of them. He wants to tell them by acting or writing.

Boseman tries to use his fame for the greater good. When *Black Panther* was in theaters, he bought all 312 tickets for one show. He gave the tickets to **underprivileged**

Fun Fact

The Black Panther character first appeared in Marvel comic books in 1966.

kids in his hometown. They would not have been able to see the movie otherwise. Boseman wanted to give back to his town and show the kids a black superhero on-screen.

Black Panther Costumes

Ruth Carter was the lead costume designer for *Black Panther.* She worked with a team of 100 people. They were from South Africa, Nigeria, and other countries. She designed clothing, armor, and jewelry. Real African tribes inspired her work. She got ideas from bright masks, neck rings, and beading.

Boseman's costume was too tight at first. He could barely breathe. So, Carter changed it. Then Boseman said it felt like a second skin. His suit blends in with the dark. It makes his character look **stealthy** and ninja-like.

Black Panther's costume is black and skintight.

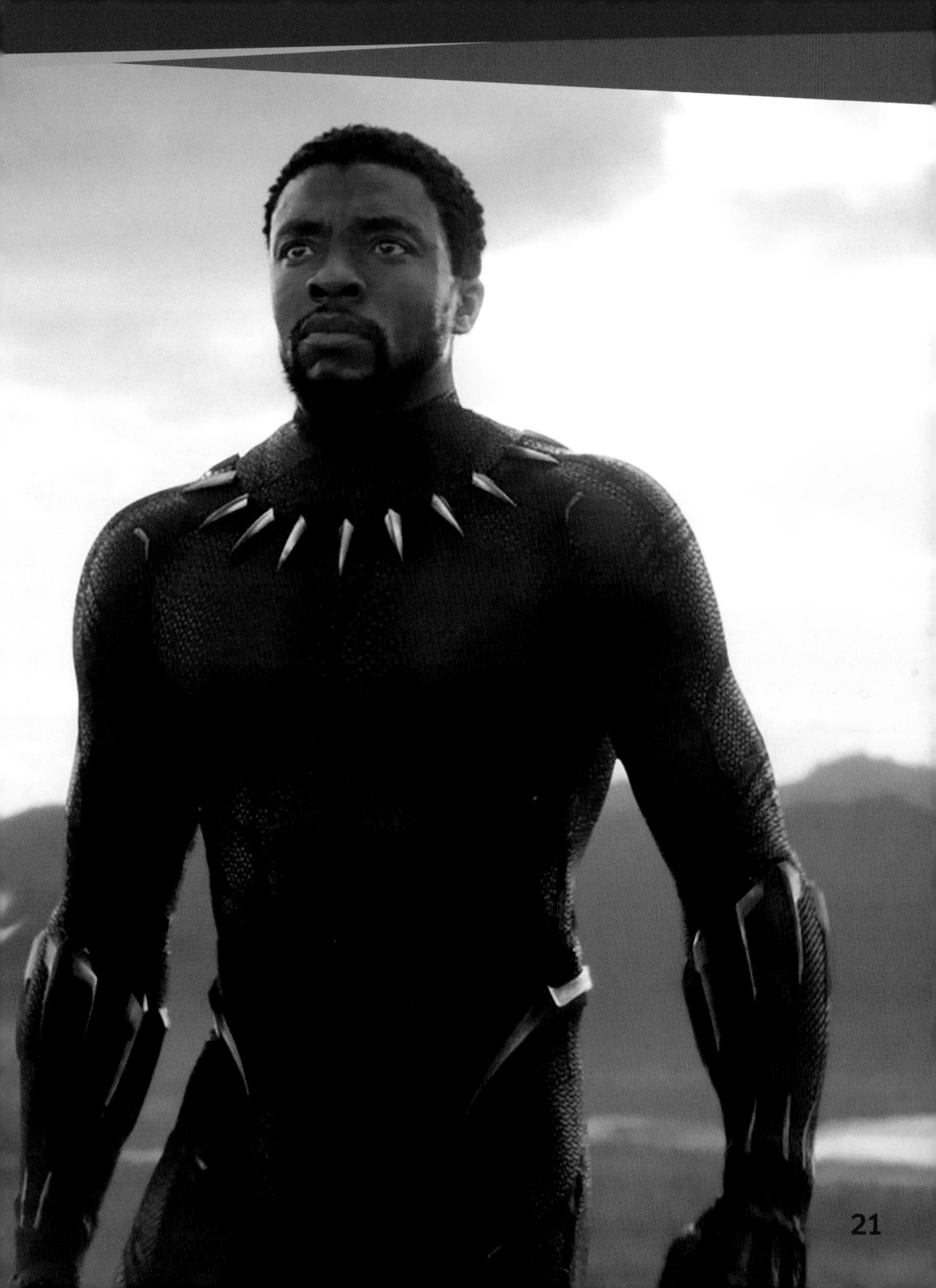

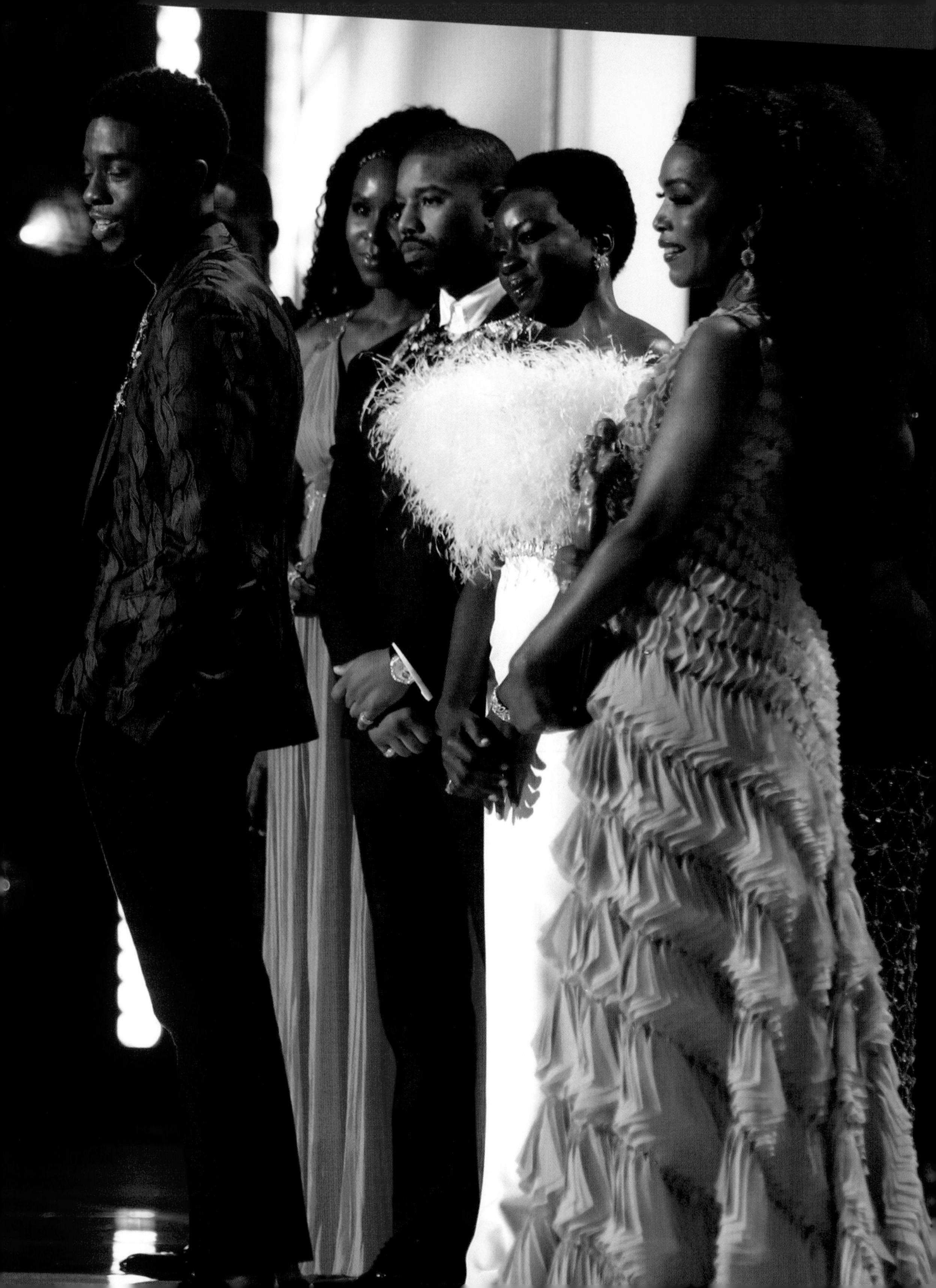

Chapter 4

The World of Wakanda

Black Panther was the first Marvel movie with a mostly black cast. It was very popular in theaters. It made $1.3 billion in ticket sales around the world. It also won three Oscars at the 2019 awards show.

Black Panther cast members accept the Screen Actors Guild Award for best cast in 2019.

The movie was filmed in Georgia. But much of the story is set in the made-up country of Wakanda. Before filming, Boseman and many others traveled to Africa. They went to learn. They studied traditional African images and sounds. They wanted Wakanda to be based on

Fun Fact

Actors who play characters from Wakanda speak with a Xhosa accent. Xhosa is an official language of South Africa.

> In *Black Panther*, the cast wears colorful blankets like the Basotho people of Southern Africa.

real African tribes. They combined what they learned with **futuristic** set pieces to create Wakanda.

The setting of Wakanda is not real. But they hoped it would feel real.

Black Panther's first on-screen appearance was in 2016. Marvel began work on a *Black Panther* **sequel** in 2019. The movie had the same director. Boseman returned as Black Panther. Many other

Fun Fact

Boseman trained in African martial arts for *Black Panther*. He learned Dambe boxing, Zulu stick fighting, and Angolan **capoeira**.

 The *Black Panther* cast attends the NAACP Image Awards, which celebrates people of color.

cast members also came back.

They looked forward to returning

to Wakanda.

FOCUS ON
Chadwick Boseman

Write your answers on a separate piece of paper.

1. Write a sentence summarizing the main ideas of Chapter 3.

2. If you were an actor, would you want to do your own stunts? Why or why not?

3. When did Boseman write his first play?

    A. He wrote it after college.

    B. He wrote it in high school.

    C. He wrote it after *Black Panther.*

4. How might experience as an actor make someone a better director?

    A. The person could see the challenges actors deal with.

    B. The person could learn a new language.

    C. The person could have more free time.

5. What does **pounce** mean in this book?

*He waits for the right moment to **pounce**. Then he jumps.*

    A. step backward

    B. remain in one place

    C. leap onto something

6. What does **inspired** mean in this book?

*Real African tribes **inspired** her work. She got ideas from bright masks, neck rings, and beading.*

    A. affected

    B. dressed up

    C. left behind

Answer key on page 32.

Glossary

capoeira
A martial art that combines elements of dance and fighting.

director
A person who is in charge of making a movie.

futuristic
Very modern or related to a future time.

Heisman Trophy
The award given to the best college football player each season.

sequel
A book or movie that continues the story of a previous book or movie.

staged
Organized and put on a play.

stealthy
Behaving in a certain way to go unnoticed.

stunts
Actions involving difficult skills or danger.

underprivileged
Not enjoying the same rights or lifestyles as the majority of people in a society.

villain
A character who works against the hero of a story.

To Learn More

BOOKS

DiPrimio, Pete. *Chadwick Boseman.* Kennett Square, PA: Purple Toad Publishing, 2018.

Hammelef, Danielle S. *Behind-the-Scenes Movie Careers.* North Mankato, MN: Capstone Press, 2017.

Santos, Rita. *Chadwick Boseman: Superstar of Black Panther.* New York: Enslow Publishing, 2018.

NOTE TO EDUCATORS

Visit **www.focusreaders.com** to find lesson plans, activities, links, and other resources related to this title.

Index

A
Africa, 20, 24–26

B
Black Panther, 5–7, 18, 20, 26
Black Panther, 7, 18, 20, 23, 26

C
Carter, Ruth, 20
Crossroads, 10

D
director, 10, 13, 26

E
Express, The, 15

H
Heisman Trophy, 15
Howard University, 10

L
Little, Floyd, 15

M
Marshall, Thurgood, 16
martial arts, 26

O
Oscars, 23

R
Robinson, Jackie, 16

S
stunts, 7

W
Wakanda, 24–27
Washington, Denzel, 11

X
Xhosa, 24